The Pocket Guide to MEN

by
Chrissie Glazebrook
and
Vanessa Trampleasure

with
Margy Cockburn
Cathy Murphy
and
Martin Butcher

Illustrations by Mollusc

Chalk & Cheese
PUBLICATIONS

First published 1986

Chalk & Cheese Publications
176 High Street
Barnet
Hertfordshire

ISBN 0 9508475 4 2

Printed in Great Britain by
The Alden Press Osney Mead Oxford
Typeset by Lineage Ltd Watford Herts

Additional material for this book was provided by:

Fran Wardell
Mary-Jane Carreyette
Marie Chinnapan
Isabel Japp
Nicholas Butcher
Caralan Eakins
Maureen Wilkes
Brian West

Cover concept by St Albans Art and Graphic Associates
Cover illustration by Royston Willcocks

INTRODUCTION

Finding the right man is a tricky business. Whether you're looking for a one-night stand or a lifetime's lover, you want a guy who'll come up with the goods. Before committing yourself to a meal, or even a drink, there are certain questions every girl wants answered. Is he rich? Is he married? Does he wash? What's he like in bed? Will he be polite to your mother? *The Pocket Guide to Men* provides the answers.

Forget the old time-consuming methods: the corny chat-up, the first-night fumbling, the let-down lay. This book means no more gambling and no more guesswork: look up the man you fancy and find out what he's *really* like.

Over forty types of men are described in intimate detail: their good points, their bad points, how to find them, how to get rid of them. And for the manhunter in a hurry, there's an instant reference system (see below) so you can tell at a glance whether the man you've got your eye on will come up to scratch.

What the symbols mean:

£ **His financial situation: is he rich, is he broke, is he *mean*? And is that his wife's Barclaycard he's using?**

Wining and dining: will he ask for his *steak tartare* to be well done or demand tomato ketchup on his *sole meunière*?

The bottom line: what's he like between the sheets? Will the earth move or will you have to fake it again?

CONTENTS

THE TRAVELLING SALESMAN

Easily spotted by his Vauxhall Cavalier with a suit jacket hanging in the back, he's surrounded by samples, polystyrene coffee cups and a well-thumbed copy of the Road Atlas of Great Britain. Wears a polyester suit with flared trousers, a Peter England shirt, tie and hankie set, and has a mark on his finger where he's taken off his wedding ring. He divides women into wives, who answer the phone and don't mind samples filling the living room, and girlfriends, who wear Cubic Zirconia jewellery and don't mind being sampled.

You'll find him in the sort of two star hotel which offers a full English Breakfast and doesn't mind 'visitors' in the bedrooms after 10pm. You'll easily attract his attention if your front looks more promising than the latest Wilbur Smith; you can then look forward to a fun packed evening of dirty jokes and discussions on the decline of the bathroom fittings market in the East Midlands. Eventually, accompanied by two warm Babychams, you'll be smuggled up to his bedroom.

£ **Tight: his income is unpredictable and he's loaded down with H.P. payments.**

Hotel Restaurant which offers 'a wide choice of International Cuisine' i.e. prawn cocktail, and duck in orange squash (or with cherry jam, £2.50 extra).

Rather unimaginative – despite having done nothing but imagine it for the last two hundred miles of the M1.

Rather unimaginative when it comes to sex, despite having done nothing but imagine it for the last two hundred miles of the M1; his performance is disturbed by a certain nervousness because the wife might ring and you're costing him more than the 10% he gets on sales.

Pros: *Not many, though at least he doesn't expect any commitment from you.*

Cons: *Adolescent and boring.*

THE AGEING HIPPY

He was christened Arthur, but prefers to be called Dylan; dresses exclusively from Oxfam – fairisle jumpers, grandad shirt, baggy cords – plus a silver marijuana leaf in his ear, which Saffron, his girlfriend (or rather 'lady') bought for him in Kashmir in 1968.

He used to be a social worker, but has given up working in favour of meditating for a better world karma. Apart from Buddhism and drugs, he enjoys making his own candles, convincing his friends he's the new Donovan with awful renditions of Mellow Yellow, writing poems about the agony of living, and listening to his huge record collection, including the complete works of the Grateful Dead.

At present, he's trying to persuade his six cats to go vegetarian and eat the lentils he puts out for them, instead of ravaging the local budgie population. He, of course, is a wholefood nut, and hopes to move to Wales to become self-sufficient on the dole. Despite vehement denials, he's been seen coming out of a McDonald's.

£ **Money's rather bourgeois, so – why don't you pay?**

Like, feel the vibrations man. Either it all hangs out or the karma's not right.

Films about the meaning of life followed by a cheapo wholefood meal, or trips in his psychedelic van to muddy pop festivals. He drinks Earl Grey tea or decaffinated coffee.

Dylan does not fuck, he makes love – no quickies on the upstairs landing. He claims his occasional failure to get it up is all down to karma, but it's probably more to do with that enormous line of speed he's just vacuumed up his nose. Will not allow himself to come until he knows the earth has moved for you.

Pros: *Loving and gentle; goes in for a lot of cuddling.*

Cons: *If you have to eat one more lentil curry…*

THE SHOWBIZ SHOW-OFF

Working for a small film company, but acting like he was Sam Goldwyn, he is entertaining, charming, great company – and a complete shit. Good looking and knows it. A perpetual womaniser, he thinks he can get a girl to drop her knickers at the drop of a famous name – and he's usually right.

Carefully scruffy and a little overweight, he stalks the trendier venues for pick-ups to further inflate his ego. You can find him at video previews, wine bars and advertising launches. In between increasingly dirty jokes, he will talk about 'these really amazing graphics for Bird's strawberry-flavour custard'. May approach you with his business card and ask if you're a model.

Wears dark glasses in candle-lit restaurants, where he will entertain you using his wife's Barclaycard. He appears wealthy but his lifestyle makes him

£ **It's his wife's money he's spending – or else he's doing it on expenses. Either way he won't spend more than is necessary to get you into bed.**

Cheap and cheerful; he won't wine and dine you at all if he thinks you'll sleep with him anyway.

He knows what he's doing, but is more interested in his satisfaction than yours. And it would help if he could remember your name...

broke. After wining and dining you, which gets more basic each time he sees you, it's back to your place. However, you may find that the girl he laid at lunchtime has exhausted him. If you persevere, you will soon find yourself treated as the supplier of a handy town pad and a sock washing service.

Pros: *Entertaining and amusing.*

Cons: *He somehow conned a good looking girl with money into marrying him; no matter how much of a stunner you are you will never be able to compete with the homely charms of her bank balance.*

THE REAL ALE FANATIC

Peering through his long, lank greasy hair to check the condition of his beer, the Real Ale Fanatic sports an extra large Arran sweater (too large even for his paunch), baggy cords, scruffy trainers and a beard matted with stale booze.

Found in nicotine stained pubs selling 27 kinds of real ale, he believes that wine bars and lager are for pouftahs and women. His opening lines include 'How's your specific gravity tonight?' and 'Like to try my Winter Warmer?' You'll be expected to keep pace with the drinking pint for pint; under no circumstances ask for a Malibu & Coke or a Special Bitter with a dash of blackcurrant.

If you survive this encounter, you'll be dragged half way round London in search of Scruggle's Traditional Sheep Dip Ale. He'll embarrass you by arguing in front of the landlord about gas pressure and specific gravity, he refuses to accept any drink not in a straight glass and moans on and on about multi-national breweries and the decline of traditional pub games. If you're still listening, he'll babble on about his hobbies – home brewing, morris dancing and compiling a guide to extinct British breweries.

£ **It's all, of course, spent on beer – he wouldn't want to waste money on you.**

Fish and chips in his scruffy bedsit.

Drunken and unimaginative – and he may end up being sick.

He's better at telling jokes about sex than actually doing it; you'll be so pissed anyway that you won't notice when he falls on top of you. Even if he succeeds in undressing and getting it up, it won't last long and he'll soon be snoring peacefully.

Pros: *Good training for aspiring alcoholics.*

Cons: *Will ruin your figure and rot your brain.*

THE INCURABLE ROMANTIC

He can spout sixteen stanzas of Wordsworth at the drop of a lace edged handkerchief, but don't worry: if you swoon at his poetic prowess, he'll produce a phial of smelling salts to revive you from the vapours. He's given to extravagant gestures, so expect to see a full-page declaration of his love in the local paper on Valentine day, or a white Corniche arriving to pick you up for a date. And his account at Interflora isn't just for special occasions – the fact it's Wednesday is reason enough to send a bouquet. Alternatively, he'll present a bunch of hand-picked, wilting cornflowers, the first of the season, 'to match your eyes'. Even a fish and chip supper is something special: he'll have a magnum of Bollinger on ice (the perfect accompaniment to battered cod) and a tiny pink rose wedged between the salt and vinegar.

Be prepared for phone calls at 3am 'just to say I'm holding the glove you left here and missing you'; it'll be some time before you leave anything more

£ **Until his book of love poetry's published, he'll find it hard to afford all those flowers; will scrimp and save to buy you presents for every conceivable occasion.**

Usually lovesick and suffering from loss of appetite, but will gaze at you dewy-eyed as you gorge yourself on oysters and champagne.

Don't attempt a post-coital fag or fall asleep – you're expected to lie cuddling and whispering sweet nothings till morning.

intimate behind. If you do persuade him to drag you off your pedestal and into bed, he'll insist you climax at least three times before he does. In the morning you'll find a dew-kissed rose on your pillow with a gilt-edged thank-you note.

You may eventually be overcome with an urge to shock him back to reality – try saying 'Fancy seeing Rambo tonight?'

Pros: *He makes you feel like a lady, even when you've just been roused from your pit with last night's mascara smeared down your cheeks.*

Cons: *He'll put you on a pedestal and worship at your feet, but can't understand there are times when you'd rather behave like a slut.*

THE SLOB

There comes a time when we all want to slum it a bit – to really be a slut, put our critical faculties on hold and hump with the first thing that hoves into view: enter The Slob. Slouched over what's left of the booze at a queue-here-for-the-bog-and-there's-no-lock-on-it type party, his feet trailing in a puddle of spilt beer, discarded fag ends, crumpled paper cups (saved from the last party) and broken red light bulbs, The Slob raises his head to sneeze over you as you pass, gives a loud burp then wipes his nose on the back of his hand – which he may then lick clean.

Assuming you were pissed enough, you'll come to in his bed (or possibly fall out of it as there's one leg missing), awakened by irregular grunts from your side and the rumble of trains passing three feet below the window. When he finally emerges into consciousness he'll make no pretence at remembering your name, but just roll on top of you for an early morning premature ejaculation while subjecting you to his own unique speciality: the ability to fart loudly simultaneously with climax.

The Slob thinks personal hygiene is for pooftahs and pansies, hence the rich farmyard fragrance of his bedsit, the unusual growths emerging from the washing-up bowl and what appears to be a complete history of the British takeaway littering

£ **Can't find his wallet so expects you to pay.**

Do not accept offers to cook you a meal.

Don't try anything fancy, like licking his ears (do not even *look* in his ears).

the floor. He cares a great deal about his appearance, spending years soiling an item before it's ready to wear socially, and carefully checking before wearing that it hasn't had its annual visit to the launderette.

Under no circumstances let him meet your family: his idea of the social graces is downing a gin and tonic in one, picking his nose between courses, telling your grandmother she has a great pair of tits, and then, thinking he is producing the final complimentary burp, throwing up all over the carpet.

Pros: *None.*

Cons: *Could permanently damage your self-respect.*

THE SUGAR DADDY

This is the man who wants the best of everything and can afford to pay for it. He's at the top of his profession, his mortgage paid off, his kids married off, his wife browned off: all the ingredients of an impending mid-life crisis. You, and Grecian 2000, can help avert it.

Usually found downing gin and tonics over a six course lunch, he keeps one eye on the stock market and the other on the look out for talent. He likes shares that perform and women that do likewise: he's looking for something frivolous and decorative to ease the strain of board meetings. The only bulge in his pocket you're interested in is his wallet: to get your sticky fingers on it, you'll need to be about his eldest daughter's age but with bigger boobs, a pert bum, tarty make-up and the ability to revive his jaded palate and flagging physique.

He'll wine and dine you in style, but without unnecessary extravagance. He introduces you to his more conservative business colleagues as his niece, and buys you expensive but unimaginative presents (or gets his secretary to: she's used to it). But you can forget the Mayfair apartment, Porsche and diamond bracelet – he'd never swing *that* with the Inland Revenue.

£ **Talk to him soothingly while you stroke his credit cards.**

He likes everything flambéed, so watch your eyelashes.

Lie back and think of the Bank of England.

He's flattered by the idea of having a mistress, and the very furtiveness of the affair excites him, sometimes even long enough to sustain an erection. With you, he can do all those things he's read about in *Playboy* ... well, maybe not *all*. He'll be eager to make love in the en suite shower, and is just dying to lap champers from your navel (could be tricky if you're ticklish). His biggest kick is ringing his wife from the hotel bedroom with you draped all over him.

Pros: *You'll be taken on holidays to the Bahamas ...*

Cons: *... and left to catch the bus home from Heathrow.*

THE MEDICAL STUDENT

Found hunting in packs at nurses' parties and real ale pubs, the Medical Student is fit but spotty; all that squash and rugby may stop him getting fat, but a diet of takeaways and hospital canteen stodge isn't doing his complexion any good. In between drinking and chasing women, they can be found running round with bits from the anatomy lab, or amusing themselves by wedging pickled willies in train doors.

Nurses are just a routine screw; any female who doesn't work in the hospital is a status symbol to be shown off to his mates – impressing them is more important than impressing you.

Chatting up will be perfunctory: in-jokes and dirty stories. Pausing only to spill a little beer over you, and to make sure his mates are watching, he'll drag you off to his scruffy digs in the secondhand sports car his dad bought him.

£ **Most of his grant (and Daddy's allowance) is spent on booze, not you.**

Very limited – takeaways and late-night curries to soak up the alcohol.

May have a nice body to compensate for his lack of technique.

When it comes to the crunch he'll play up being pissed to cover up his inadequacy. He knows all the Latin terms for the naughty bits, but is a hopeless lover; he may just lie there and ask you to tickle his vas deferens. He'll joke about cunnilingus and fellatio rather than actually do it. Ends up being sick or falling asleep.

Pros: *The prospect of a profitable practice in Harley Street...*

Cons: *...if you can stand the adolescent antics.*

THE SHY MAN

Happiest when he's at home playing with his Hornby train set, he hasn't been out with a girl for years. He once tried chatting up a check-out girl at Tesco's, but was overcome with embarrassment. The downcast eyes, chewed-up fingernails and fumbling for his purse may not be very sexy, but he'll be pathetically grateful for the fact that you've talked to him at all. He's not so much a man, more of a lost puppy you want to pick up and cuddle.

He'll either be living with his mother, or all alone in a place-for-everything-and-everything-in-its-place flat. Mummy comes in to clean it once a week since deciding that, at the age of 28, he was old enough to live on his own.

To get his attention, you'll have to try to get him drunk on lemonade shandy and persuade him to tell you about his one and only passion: toy train sets; with luck, he'll invite you home to see his 'Rocket'. Back at his place, offer to make the coffee (make it strong – about 50% vodka) while he sets up the signal box. If he comments on the taste, tell him the milk was on the turn.

£ **Doesn't earn much, but would hate you to know it. Will be overcome with embarrassment if you offer to pay.**

Don't take him anywhere with intimidating wine waiters, incomprehensible menus, or dancing on the tables.

You're totally in charge. With encouragement, he'll do whatever you want, thinking it's frightfully naughty – he never knew girls could be like this.

Once you've lured him away from the sidings and on to the sofa, he'll fumble with your bra straps while apologising for his inexperience. He says he's a terrible lover – he's dead right.

The best bit is the cuddle afterwards: he'll be affectionate, grateful and, just like those rare occasions when friends asked him round for tea, he'll thank you for having him. Resist the temptation to reply 'Thank you for coming' or 'Do come again'.

Pros: *Can be romantic, affectionate and refreshingly naive.*

Cons: *Once the novelty wears off, you may feel an urge for an ungracious, uncouth but definitely randy rogue.*

THE MENOPAUSAL MALE

Having a last fling at the age of 45, he's splashed out on a new wardrobe of designer jeans, fluffy jumpers, sexy undies and a new hair piece; may add contact lenses, trainers and a finishing touch of expensive but unpleasant aftershave.

He started to come to terms with creeping old age at his son's eighteenth birthday party; not only did he learn that Duran Duran were not a firm of solicitors, but his attempts to jitter-bug to Paul Young brought the house down.

Can be found in discos frequented by German tourists and secretaries with complimentary tickets; after ten Pina Coladas he manages to do the Watootsie to a stream of obscure soul numbers. He had hoped to pick up a dolly bird, but ends up with Beryl whose old man is a long distance lorry driver.

£ **Earns a lot but it all goes on school fees and the mortgage. Feels guilty about splashing out on you.**

He's concerned about his waistline and about being seen with you; he'd prefer to drag you off to bed before you change your mind.

Somewhat unnerved if you're demanding or adventurous, he's worried about getting home and it will all be over pretty quickly.

Worried about his health and trying to lose weight, he has acquired a trendy track suit to go jogging round Haywards Heath. Has given up eating butter and is trying to live off muesli, skimmed milk and gin & tonic. Entered the London Marathon and came in 13,579th.

Pros: *Not many, though he does know how to treat a lady in an old-fashioned way (i.e. spend money on her).*

Cons: *Sex: Will be too embarrassed to take his teeth out so expect a few surprises. Does what his wife likes – can't remember, or has never done, anything else.*

THE RUGBY PLAYER

This is probably the only man for whom you could supply an extensive description of the spots on his backside before you are even afforded a formal introduction. He's a gregarious animal, always in a pack, and never without a song on his lips or a dribble of beer down his shirt. For Rugby Players, hunting for women is a bit like the scrum – you're all in it together and you grab the first thing that moves.

He's basically a man's man, so if you've set your sights on him you'll need an A-level in tolerance and marked masochistic tendencies. You'll have to get used to standing ankle deep in mud, in a biting wind, watching thirty grown men chase an oval piece of inflated leather up and down a wet field. Rugby is a game which defies logic or explanation, so never make the mistake of pretending you understand the rules.

After the match comes the club house booze-up, a riot of ribald songs and incomprehensible party games. Stand in wonderment as your man releases a crotchful of pennies into a bucket. Marvel as he crawls spread-eagled across the floor clutching a couple of Newcastle Brown bottles.

£ **Drinking his way through a fortune.**

Liquid refreshment only.

If you're lucky, you may see his prop forward once a week. Pre-match he'll stay celibate to preserve his strength, post match he'll most likely to be unconscious – this could be why rugby players seldom score a goal, only a try.

Heave a sigh as he sinks into a coma at the end of another night's alcohol abuse. You're expected to watch from the sidelines, handing him the condoms to blow up, and then driving him home when he's too rat-arsed to find the car park.

If he's still conscious when you haul him into bed, he may stun you with a display of his world famous Fart Flares. Foreplay consists of giving him a blow job to restore the booze-affected member; as soon as it's even semi-rigid – wham, it's in. And for your apres-ejaculation treat, further examples of his fart projection prowess – this time with him fully comatose.

Pros: *He may look the essence of masculinity...*

Cons: *... but proving his manhood could be more difficult.*

THE HYPOCHONDRIAC

Hairless, wimp-like and accident prone, The Hypochondriac is a neurotic bundle of nerves. He smothers his face in Savlon if he cuts himself shaving and washes his hands in Dettol after having a pee. If you've got a headache, he's got a brain tumour, and if he catches 'flu he thinks it's malaria.

It's quite difficult to meet The Hypochondriac. He feels it's probably safer to work from home, and he's not much of a socialiser (all those germs!) An evening out fills him with anxiety: it's so difficult to know where to go. A pub? He can't stand cigarette smoke and doesn't drink alcohol. A cosy dinner for two in a candlelit restaurant? He won't eat funny foreign food and insists on inspecting the kitchen.

Perhaps *you* had better cook for him. You'll need to spring clean your flat (he'll notice dust your mother wouldn't spot), and choose the menu carefully. He's terrified of salmonella so he won't eat poultry, seafood doesn't agree with him and he's allergic to meat: lettuce on toast is probably about right. Whatever you prepare, remember that he likes his food cooked to destruction – don't try reheating those leftover prawns …

£ **His life membership of B.U.P.A. has set him back a bit.**

Have you tried getting drunk on Perrier water?

At least you know you won't catch something.

Sex, of course, is tricky. He insists on pure cotton sheets (he's allergic to man-made fibres) and will suggest you go and have a bath first. He wears a sheath for *his* protection and is fastidious about foreplay: he won't lick whipped cream off your nipples, but might agree to rub your back with antiseptic lotion. He's not into buggery of course, and won't kiss your naughty bits. He'll offer 'His' and 'Hers' towels for après-sex wipey-poohs, but don't expect any cosy post-coital chatting: he'll probably say 'I don't feel very well ... have you got any paracetamol?' before rushing off to wash his willy in Domestos.

Pros: *It makes a nice change to have a man who's fastidious.*

Cons: *Only trouble is he makes* ***you*** *feel dirty.*

THE LOVABLE ROGUE

With his Jack Nicholson looks, effortless banter and winning smile, The Lovable Rogue can get away with murder – or at least cuddling up to you in bed while telling you all about one of his many other conquests. A devil with an angelic grin, he tramples over you and tells you whopping great lies, but all with such wide-eyed innocence that you just have to believe him.

It's your birthday, and he's promised you dinner at the most expensive restaurant in town. You spend hours getting ready. You knew he'd be late picking you up but, by midnight, you know he's stood you up again. You spend a tearful night cursing him and resolve that this is definitely The End.

Next day he turns up with a dozen red roses, a disarming smile and an implausible yarn about taking his maiden aunt to a Cliff Richard concert. Before you know it you're between the sheets, melting in his practised embrace, all your good intentions forgotten.

In reality of course he picked up one of your friends in the local wine bar and took *her* for a meal. But you don't find that out till much, much later.

£ **Running a harem's an expensive business: he has almost as many credit cards as he does women.**

 **Greeted as an old friend at restaurants he's 'never been to before'.**

 **Shows a marked dislike of love bites and back scratching.**

The Lovable Rogue has a healthy sexual appetite (though he tends to go for quantity rather than quality), three little black books and a 32k memory, all essential for a man trying to keep a string of women happy.

At parties, he flirts with all the females while still managing to convey that you're a little bit special. He'll present you with a hand-made Swiss chocolate Easter egg – from a bulk pack of twelve. He'll bring the finest dressed crab for your cat – eleven other well-fed moggies wait expectantly for *their* treat.

You'd never buy a used car from this man – but you buy his love-lies every time.

Pros: *You know he's a womaniser ...*

Cons: *... but you can't resist his charm.*

THE TV ADDICT

Pale, spotty and over-weight, The TV Addict has an almost totally sedentary lifestyle. His only exercise is staggering to the nearest bus stop on the way to his job as a computer programmer; he happily sits in front of a VDU all day, but gets in a panic if he thinks he won't be home in time for *Crossroads*.

The moment he gets home he rushes in to check that the video has recorded *Afternoon Plus*, to be watched in the small hours after *The Epilogue* or *The Open University* have finished.

The TV Addict has little time for women. Quite apart from the time-consuming demands of his hobby, no real life woman can match the glamorous painted goddesses of *Dynasty* or *Dallas*, or the larger than life loud-mouths of *East Enders* and *Coronation Street*.

His ideal woman is probably a wholesome but sexy girl-next-door type, in the Ann Diamond or Pamela Armstrong mould. But somehow one feels they might not fancy an overweight thirty-year-old with TV dinner stains down his BHS pullover. They've even stopped answering his fan mail.

The highspot of his TV watching career was having two lines of a letter read out on *Points of View*, complaining about yet another repeat of

£ **Saving up for a 36″ screen stereo hi-fi TV with built-in freezer and microwave oven.**

 **Takeaways from round the corner, or Vesta TV dinners.**

 **Only possible if there is nothing of interest on the telly, like the test card.**

Postman Pat. His favourite programme is *It'll Be All Right On The Night*; he mourns the passing of live television when he could gleefully point out a microphone creeping into view on *Z Cars*.

Now he contents himself with explaining the technological wizardry behind the production of the weather map, and you may even get taken to a recording of *The Cilla Black Show*, complete with running commentary: 'Now that man waving his arms about, he's the floor manager and ...'

Pros: *Good chance to catch up on your beauty sleep as you doze quietly through Channel 4 documentaries on basket making in Uruguay.*

Cons: *An unfortunate tendency to forget your name, and call you Sue Ellen or Alexis.*

THE BEACH ROMEO

A magnificent physical specimen who flaunts his constant tan, pumped-up biceps, buttocks tight as ticks and well-developed muscles – with one particularly intimate muscle cleverly arranged for maximum effect. Dark-eyed, with long eyelashes and well flossed teeth, the Caribbean species will be doused from head to foot in Hawaiian Tropic Professional Tanning Oil. The Costa del Sol variety prefers to be soaked in Brut, though this tends to dissolve the gold plating on his chunky-style neck chain.

Found on any holiday beach, disguised perhaps as an ice cream vendor or water ski instructor, he's easily attracted by any suitable bait (brown, blonde, big boobs and not too intelligent looking). His appetite is large and he's not fussy whether he lands you or your friend.

Conversation will be limited, but all of it flattering and very much to the point. Don't expect to be

£ **Limited – parading up and down the beach may be his full-time occupation.**

Basic but fun: drinks on the beach or a cheap and cheerful disco.

Experienced and uninhibited – could make your man back home seem just a teensy bit boring.

wined and dined in style: he's expecting to impress you with the contents of his swimming trunks, not his wallet.

Pros: *His lack of costume allows you to check his attributes before you get involved; he looks good on holiday snaps, is a useful accessory to summer fashions and a definite boost to the ego.*

Cons: *His charms do not transport well – what looked cute on the Costa Brava can seem out of place on the London Underground. He's best left at the airport – and make sure you only bring back souvenirs you cherish.*

THE FUDDY DUDDY

This is a man who was born middle-aged. He sends away for holiday brochures on Boxing Day to ensure he gets the same hotel as last year, and has yellow-fever shots for a jaunt to Jersey. Before he leaves, he'll do three laps of the house to check that everything is turned off. He keeps a fire extinguisher and thermal blanket in his car, and a spare set of keys attached by magnet under the wheel arch. He's dying to buy a video, but wouldn't dream of committing himself before consulting *Which?*

His idea of decadence is lying in bed on Sunday morning listening to the omnibus edition of *The Archers*. When he gets up he'll wear a velour dressing-gown with cord belt over his paisley pyjamas. And don't think you can serve lasagne for Sunday lunch. He's strictly a meat-and-two-veg man. If you do eat out, he'll never take you to an Oriental restaurant – he likes to know what he's eating. He's wary of 'foreign' food like aubergines, and always orders Blue Nun to drink.

In bed, it's strictly sex by numbers. He'll spend a set number of minutes on ear-blowing, nipple-nibbling and gentlemanly stroking of your intimate

£ **Very careful. He's been with the same bank and building society since he was eighteen.**

Anywhere the menu is printed in English.

Predictable – and always in the missionary position.

parts. That's as adventurous as he'll get – he thinks oral sex only happens in France.

He buys his shirts in threes – all the same – from Austin Reed. You may also see him in the cash-and-carry buying catering jars of Horlicks, or tins of Butter Osborne biscuits. He's as boring as a back-number of *Reader's Digest* at the dentist's, where he attends a check-up every six months to the day.

Pros: *He'll never stand you up or arrive late for a date…*

Cons: *… but let's face it, the man's a BORE.*

THE GAY

Gay men are so good-looking it's unfair. It seems such a waste: the most gorgeous men always turn out to be gay.

Your beautiful hairdresser; that hunky actor whose steamy sex-scenes you've replayed so often on the video; those studs you spot coming out of the local 'health club'; that thickset biker; those lone denimed or leathered figures walking their dogs on the common – none of them even give you a second glance.

It's his very unavailability that makes The Gay so appealing, and so tantalizing, and you've soon convinced yourself that you're the woman to convert him to the delights of the female sex. You tell yourself that he was over-cosseted by his mother, that he hasn't met the right woman or that it was all due to his public school education: you just can't admit that he simply doesn't fancy you.

If you persevere, you risk becoming a fag-hag – a gay groupie gazing longingly at all those perfect haircuts and perfect clothes, tagging along to parties at perfectly restored houses with perfectly prepared food, admiring the perfectly ironed napkins that match the curtains that match the cushions that match the carpet – then gazing in

£ **No wife and kids to support, so he's probably loaded.**

Elegant but pretentious – he's a bit of a foodie.

Don't hold out any hopes. If he does agree, he'll probably only be going through the motions.

amazement at seventeen bottles of aftershave in the Homes and Gardens bathroom.

But a gay can be the best male friend you've ever had. He'll understand your problems and treat you as an equal – after all, you do have a major interest in common.

You can become very fond of him, but don't ever hope to get him into bed. To have any chance at all, you'll need to be cast in the mould of a Liza Minelli or a Tina Turner, a Diana Ross or a Shirley Bassey: The Gay's got all their records, and might just love to drown in all that forceful femininity.

Pros: *A great friend ...*

Cons: *... but never a lover.*

THE SALOON BAR BORE

You'll hear him before you see him, loudly expounding his latest theory on politics or football hooliganism. 'I happen to know…' or 'The fact is…' precedes every authoritive outpouring.

His dress suggests studied but dated nonchalance – how many men do you know who still wear a cravat? The Bore's sartorial ensemble may include a Lovat tweed jacket with obligatory leather elbows, mustard-coloured waistcoat and simulated cavalry twill Sta-Prest trousers. And for the Total Look, a moustache garnished with beer froth. His car reflects his personality – loud and vulgar on the outside, but a bit short-charged under the bonnet.

To catch him, you'll have to learn to perch prettily on a bar stool and hang enthralled on his every word. You'll also have to be adept at stifling yawns – never let on about your sociology degree. He feels threatened by intelligent women and hates sociologists.

He'll trot you out at social functions like the Rotary dinner, or ladies night at the Masonic Hall, where you'll see his listeners develop glazed eyes and facial tics. At the end of an evening being the butt

---

£ **Quite well off, but likely to be spending it on a new patio or double glazing. In fact probably sells double glazing himself.**

Berni Inn, where he shows off to the waitresses or complains about everything.

Useless, and he'll probably be drunk – you'll probably need to be too.

of sexist innuendo and hints of all-night stands to come, you'll discover the truth in the saying 'empty vessels make most noise'. They also make lousy lovers – his women are bored, not laid.

Pros: *None.*

Cons: *Prepare to become a social leper. Your friends will suddenly remember pressing engagements when you ask them for a drink. Worst of all, monumental boringness could be contagious.*

THE YUMMY YES MAN

Decisions, decisions, he can't make them so you have to. He's tall, slim, good looking – and indecisive. Are you going to see White Knights or Out of Africa? Will you eat Italian or French? Which shoes should he wear? The choice is yours. You don't like his carefully cultivated beard? He'll shave it off. You've noticed a few thinning patches? He'll have a hair transplant.

Indecisive he may be, but the Yes Man has been impeccably trained. This is the guy with four arms. Carrying flowers in one hand and an umbrella held over you with another (and it is over you – he'll be getting rained on while you, clutching your chocolates, stay beautifully dry), yet he still manages to have an arm around your waist, and another hand free to open the car door.

But of course, there's a catch. A man who panders to a woman's every need is going to be

£ **This guy's never going to be rich – but he's never going to be sacked either. He'll remember your birthday, but don't expect any lavish treats.**

You choose the restaurant, the wine, what you eat, what he eats ... and he won't have garlic without asking if you mind.

Will light you a post-coital ciggie even though he doesn't smoke.

much in demand. The female has to do the chatting up, but he's far too polite to turn a woman down. Once in bed, and you'll have to lead him there, he'll be the most thoughtful and considerate lover ('What colour condom should I wear?), but does he *always* have to ask permission before taking off your bra? He'll make the bed and bring you breakfast there, but won't even get in without asking first.

Pros: *Not so much wet as drip dry, the Yes Man can be neglected and ignored, yet come back without a crease in his smile, his manners spotless…*

Cons: *…and still wondering which brand of washing powder you think he ought to buy.*

THE DIVORCEE

A pathetic case of irretrievable breakdown, he can be spotted in launderettes where he dyes his shirts pink by boiling them with multi-coloured towels. He thought he had it made: mortgage, index-linked pension, 2.4 children. Then – zap! The little woman he'd taken for granted went to a consciousness raising group and he was out on his ear.

Now living in a bedsit in squalid chaos, he got the raw deal when the marital home was being divided. She got the Habitat futon, he got the zed-bed. She got the Mary Quant co-ordinated duvet set, he got the brushed nylon sheets the kids had poked their toes through. Settling down each evening in front of a black and white telly, eating baked beans from the tin followed by lemon curd sandwiches, he's a sad case of chronic neglect. His collars and cuffs are frayed, his shoes are down at heel. That two day growth on his chin isn't designer stubble, it's the first symptom of approaching vagrancy.

Occasionally he makes a supreme effort and drags himself to the Divorced and Separated Club, where he dances to Barry Manilow records cheek

£ **Once he's forked out for her maintenance there's not much left to spend on you. Expect to go Dutch – or pay for everything.**

Round at your place for some good home cooking. He hasn't had a square meal since the break-up.

Angst gives him potency problems. He'll either be a non-starter or a Johnny-come-quickly.

to cheek with equally desperate deserted women. He knows the gestation period and Latin name of every animal in the zoo, where he spends every Sunday with his spoiled, hyperactive children, buying them coke and ice cream and pumping them for details of their mother's private life. Drowning in self-pity and his ex-wife's debts, he's desperate for another relationship; but he's set in her ways, and you'll always feel you're being compared – and found wanting.

Pros: *He'll marry you like a shot – he's desperate for someone to look after him.*

Cons: *You'll live with the spectre of his first wife, and the awful reality of those obnoxious kids. They may even come to live with you!*

THE HACKNEY HERBERT

He runs a stall in the local market, but has a finger in several other pies; he lives with his Mum and Dad (when the old geezer is not away for a stretch) the whole family residing in a council maisonette, along with various girlfriends, boyfriends and his fifteen-year-old sister's twins.

Wearing filthy jeans and a T-shirt during the day, he likes to dress up at night in Farrah trousers, a very expensive leather jacket (just like the one on Police 5 the other day), a thirty-six inch belcher chain and half a litre of Aramis. You'll encounter him in the local theme pub; if you're the right type (high heels, short skirts, big knockers) you'll elicit his favourite chat-up line ('Ello darlin') and before you know it you'll be whisked off to a wild night at Catford dogs, followed by a Vindaloo and chips.

He can't take you home 'cos his Mum wouldn't like it; if he's sober enough to perform it'll be a grapple in the back of his tastefully decorated Capri: go-faster stripes, furry dashboard and silly stickers on the back window.

£ **He can't be earning *that* much from running a market stall…**

If he's 'done a deal' it's steak and chips; otherwise you'll have to be content with takeaways.

He'll assume you'll do it on the first night, and will expect you to be impressed by the size of his organ. Regards love bites as a status symbol.

Never mind. He's not mean with his money – you can have all the Malibu & Coke you can drink – and on your birthday you get the works: *Charlie*, gold jewellery, Berni Inn and a bottle of Mateus Rosé. And when the muzak's playing his favourite song, *Three Times a Lady*, he'll go all dewy eyed and suggest a dirty fortnight in Benidorm. What more could a girl want?

Pros: *Refreshingly direct: none of that 'I respect you as a person' rubbish.*

Cons: *It'd be nice to get laid in a bed occasionally.*

THE NO-HOPER

Usually found totally alone in launderettes, the public bars of deserted pubs, or attending an evening class in stamp collecting at the local library. Should you be unwise enough to give him even half of a smile, he'll latch on to you for the rest of the evening, convinced that at last, after all these years, his luck has finally changed.

Once you've got over his terminal acne, you'll realise that he should not wear slim-fit shirts (he bought six, all the same, in a sale) and you'll notice that his underarm stains appear to be permanent. His flared trousers are just that bit too short, displaying the odd sock and the stack boots with the stick-on heels not quite stuck.

It's fatal to give him the slightest encouragement: all you need do is smile at him and he takes it as an invitation to shove his hands up your jumper. He spends the whole evening leering at your 'bazookas' and then expects a grapple in the car park on the way home. If you're foolish enough to accept his offer of a lift, you'll find the passenger door of his car doesn't open, he gets lost trying to take a short cut, and he finally runs out of petrol while looking for a garage that gives 2p off a gallon.

£ **He'll buy you anything you like to impress you – provided it can be bought from Woolworth's.**

Watching him eat spaghetti is like watching a wet sweater being unravelled.

You'll have to remind him to take his socks off.

If you make it back to his place, it turns out to be a chaotic bed sit which reeks of stale socks and sour milk; he calls it 'my penthouse'. You think you're lucky that there are sheets on the bed – till you look a little closer. Ignore the extra-strength foot odour powder on the bedside table, and simply relax and enjoy the sound of Leonard Cohen on the 1960's record player he bought in a jumble sale.

Three minutes of breathless sex later, he settles down to tell you his life story. He then expects you to go home (after all, you're not married – what would the landlady think?) but assumes you can't wait to see him again – by which time he'll have bragged to the entire office about his 'latest conquest'.

Pros: *He's got a heart of gold …*

Cons: *… but it's hidden beneath layers of gunge.*

THE BIKER

It all started when his Mum gave birth to him in the sidecar on the way to hospital. He was able to strip down and reassemble his tricycle at the age of six, and had defaced his school blazer with studs by the time he was nine.

Now working as a motorbike messenger, he won't hesitate to ask you out when delivering a grimy package to your office; it won't be until he takes his helmet off outside the Motorhead gig that you get any idea what he looks like.

Unable to hold a conversation due to the high decibel level of the 'music', he won't ask what you want to drink but simply present you with a pint of flat lager in a plastic glass; he'll then protectively plonk his hand on your bum, while his other hand gives your boobs what feels like full throttle.

After a hair-raising ride back to his place (having said 'yes' at the concert when you thought he was just asking if you wanted another drink) you pick your way through the bike parts on the bedroom floor; it soon becomes obvious that it's not just bikes he can strip down blindfold.

£ **Have you seen the price of Harley-Davidson spares?**

He prefers his food, like his bike, to be covered in grease and thinks coffee only tastes right out of a polystyrene cup.

What he lacks in refinement he makes up for with energy – may even take you for a 'ton'.

Afterwards, with a can of warm beer in one hand and an Old Holborn roll-up in the other, you realise that what you originally thought were black satin sheets were once white cotton, and you notice assorted grey grease marks all over your body (well, some of it anyway – he's not into elaborate foreplay).

If you're going to continue this relationship, you'll just have to invest in a bulk supply of Swarfega and a set of industrial quality nail brushes.

Pros: *Has his own transport and doesn't notice if your hair's in a mess or your flat looks a tip.*

Cons: *Leaves his dirty leathers all over your white linen sofa; your washing bills will escalate, and he'll require sandpapering down before meeting your parents.*

THE OFFICE WOLF

Sporting an M & S slimfit shirt, slightly flared pinstripe trousers and a gaudy polyester tie from C & A, the Office Wolf introduces himself with 'Hello sweetheart, if your typewriter needs adjusting' nudge, nudge, wink, wink, 'I'm your man, know what I mean?' Convinced he's God's gift to women, he lives and breathes sex to the exclusion of everything else. Spends most of his time lurking near the ladies' toilets, bumping into you in the corridor or joining you uninvited in the canteen to play footsie under the table.

Describes himself as the 'Office Services Executive', which means ordering the paper clips and refilling the Tampax machine. Contrives to make replenishing your carbon paper supplies the occasion for pinching your bum and peering down your cleavage. He may seem nice at first, but it's fatal to show any interest or you'll find two clammy hands on your boobs while he's 'mending your typewriter'.

£ **Pretends to earn more than he does – and may have a wife and kids to support.**

Very limited – having dragged you to the pub there's only one thing on his mind. Wouldn't know where to take you for a meal and he might miss the last train home.

Despite his boastings, he's more used to talking about it than actually doing it. Not recommended.

Highspot of the year is the office party; he'll endeavour to get you even drunker than he is while standing so close that you get condensation down your cleavage, followed by a sweaty palm and accompanied by 'I've always liked you, Jane ... oh ... Sarah, well, like I was saying, I've always liked you and...'

Pros: *Once he's accepted you don't fancy him he can become a useful friend.*

Cons: *Difficult to put him off – a Herpes Clinic appointment card on your desk is often the only answer.*

THE AGEING POP STAR

Born on a council estate somewhere Oop North, he was once the fresh faced idol of millions of screaming teenyboppers. Now practically a recluse, he lives in isolated splendour in an eighteenth century mansion, the proud owner of acres of farmland that are now going to seed as rapidly as he is.

With no expense spared, he has constructed a custom-designed recording studio, where he lays down computer-arranged tracks for his new concept album – five years in the making and still no release date.

He made a big thing about weaning himself off drugs in the seventies, having been permanently stoned for years. He tried eastern mysticism (until his guru was imprisoned for grand larceny) and is now a born-again millionaire.

He occasionally leaves his stately home to appear at a miners' benefit gig or to record a track on an anti-apartheid album. He may even appear on an upmarket chat show, in a grimy designer shirt, symmetrically ripped denims and hand made clogs, to talk about his political opinions and his concern for Swedish rain forests. Meanwhile, he shows his concern for his erstwhile fans by turning

£ **He *did* have loads, but does seem to be getting through it rather quickly.**

In public: organically grown wholefoods. In private: jam butty and chips.

Finds it hard to live up to his former sexy image, but he still thinks it's a privilege to go to bed with him.

up two hours late for occasional mega-gigs at Wembley stadium, where he discovers he can no longer play the three chord riff that made him famous.

He may even make the odd film. Despite thousands spent on media hype, it turns out to be a spectacular box office flop. But never mind, his accountants will be pleased – he needed a gigantic tax loss.

Pros: *You might get your picture in the gossip columns.*

Cons: *He still expects to be hero worshipped.*

THE TRADESMAN

If you like service with a smile, this is your man. He's an opportunist on the lookout for a spot of suburban nookie, so be on your guard when he turns up with a cheeky grin, and says that he's come to tinker with your plumbing. *Never* open the door in your nightie, offer him a coffee before he starts work or say you're popping upstairs to make the bed. To him, these are invitations to a spot of illicit overtime – in his haste to rip off his dungarees he'll probably botch the job he came to do in the first place.

Only happy when he's on the job, he preys on bored women, and he's not fussy where he sinks his plumb-line. Succumb, and you have problems: tradesmen have a jungle drum system. If you monkey about with one wrench, you'll find a constant stream of boiler-suited Lotharios offering you a quick overhaul. And don't expect a reduction: your two hours of afternoon delight will be charged at time-and-a-half and added to your bill. Add the cost of removing grease marks from the duvet cover, and it could turn out to be an expensive service.

He has this notion that every woman likes a bit of

£ **Only too willing to accept payment in kind.**

May invite you to share his fish paste sandwiches and Thermos of tea.

Unpredictable – he may prefer to use the tradesman's entrance.

rough now and again, and that they're attracted by ingrained grime, dirty fingernails, and male perspiration. He may throw you a few come-on lines: corny, oft-repeated double entendres about screws, tools and customer satisfaction. Your best response is to say your husband is a professional boxer and will be home any minute.

If he *does* catch you out when you're feeling horny, don't draw the bedroom curtains and make sure his van's parked well out of sight.

Pros: *Useful if your system needs emergency treatment …*

Cons: *… but you may end up with the central heating still not working.*

THE LIBERATED MAN

You go to consciousness-raising group, while he stays home ironing his hand-spun hair shirts. You come home whacked from your Open University tutorial – he has a steaming courgette casserole ready. He even buys two Guardians so there's no argument over the crossword.

But let's not mince words. He's a bit wet, isn't he? Liberation may have made you believe in role-sharing, but deep down you still want to be dominated. The once-masterful, macho male has degenerated into a creche-minding wimp. Admit it, he looks ridiculous in his bio-degradable dungarees, harvesting the alfalfa sprouts and checking the temperature of the tofu. Don't you just long for him to pin you against the stripped pine and give you a table-ender?

But he'll never do it. He's so determined everything must be equitable he won't have an orgasm until you've faked yours. He'll insert your diaphragm, or check your vaginal mucus to ensure you're in the safe period; if he asks "How was it for you?" once more you'll throttle him. Liberated Man is so caring he insists on spending the afterglow on the wet patch in the bed.

You'll spend your holidays at vegetarian guesthouses in the Cotswolds where the

£ **His earnings from the wholefood co-operative are in a joint account with the Ecology Building Society; he won't spend a farthing without consulting you.**

Macrobiotic, naturally.

He insists on equality in everything, so there should be plenty of soixante-neuf.

organically-grown produce is served with due consideration for yin and yang. Secretly you'd love ten days in Benidorm, gorging paella, guzzling Sangria, and cheerfully vomiting your way back to the half-built hotel.

A by-product of the women's movement, Liberated Man is sneered at by men, despised by radical Wimmin, and eventually looked down on by you.

How can you respect a man who treks round the shops looking for the best buy in natural sponge tampons?

Pros: *You can always nip off for a bit of nookie with the milkman. Liberated Man will accept that this is all part of living in your own space.*

Cons: *His consciousness has been raised so much his head is in the clouds. If he doesn't assert himself soon you'll strangle him with his pinny.*

THE LABOURER

Whistling at you from above from his vantage point on the scaffolding, or looking up your skirt from a hole in the road, The Labourer enjoys a view of you denied to other men. But he's fussy about where he turns his attentions; his ideal woman is young, slim and flaunts all the stereotype pointers: high heels, tight skirts, low-cut acrylic jumpers and tarty make-up. He's well-built and attractively dirty, his top half bare, dusty and tanned. His faded denims are belted low and loose over his haunches; the crotch is crudely patched, as if to suggest that the jeans alone aren't man enough to contain the mighty beast that stirs within.

He doesn't say much, and won't expect you to either; instead, he boasts an extensive repertoire of well-practised body-talk: it's all stance, gestures, whistles and winks. He struts, three floors up on the scaffolding, with one thumb hooked inside his front belt loop: *Here's mine, now show me yours.*

If you accept this intriguing invitation, it's unlikely to be preceded by more than a night in the pub, complete with strippers. He may park you in a corner with a sticky drink while he brags to his mates about his latest conquest, or simply sit and leer while he gets you drunk.

£ **Provided it's pay day there'll be no expense spared.**

He's already had his tea and it's now time for drinking.

Good, honest thrusting and he does have a lovely body. But none of those strange continental practices – like foreplay.

If, or rather when, it comes to sex location may be a problem: he's either married or still living with Mum and Dad – he may suggest you use the back of his Transit. However, he has plenty of stamina, is repetitive (in the nicest possible way) though he tends to lack finesse: he thinks foreplay is a new system for the horses. Don't expect to be recognised the next day: the building's going up and his attentions have moved on.

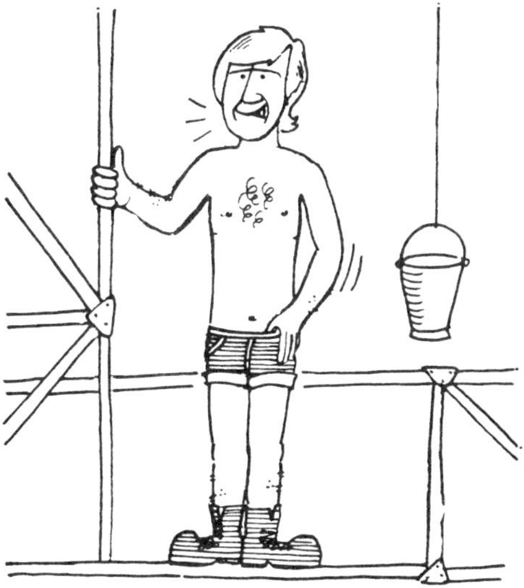

Pros: *Gorgeous to have on top of you.*

Cons: *He treats all women the same: if he fancies them they're a sex machine, if he marries them they're a domestic servant.*

THE MIDDLE-AGED TRENDY

He clumps around on Cuban heels. His hair – what's left of it – will be cunningly redistributed à la Arthur Scargill, teased, back-combed, and so heavily sprayed a tornado wouldn't budge it. The obligatory medallion nestles in his greying chest hair, or for the more cosmopolitan, a 9-carat cocaine spoon. On his wrist, liver spots and a Hong Kong replica of a Rolex Oyster. His Hawaiian shirt will be open to the navel, displaying years of alcohol abuse centred on his paunch. Round what used to be his waist, a Gucci belt holds up a pair of white designer jeans, slightly flared, as he thinks they're more flattering.

He's been taking disco dance lessons at the local church hall, and flails his flabby limbs around like a geriatric John Travolta. Occasionally he lapses into the Twist or the Locomotion, circa early Sixties, his heyday if he ever had one.

His bachelor pad is a shrine to kitsch. In the corner, a quilted dralon cocktail bar, complete with olives, blue Bols, pink elephants and tinsel umbrellas. His record collection proudly shows Fine Young Cannibals and Simply Red. Dig deeper and you'll come across Engelbert Humperdink and the odd Max Bygraves.

£ **He spends so much on moisturiser, medallions and Malibu, there's precious little left for you.**

Somewhere lit with candles to play down his wrinkles; pretentious and tacky, where he can show off his prowess with chopsticks.

He keeps up to date with the latest sex manuals, but while the spirit is willing the flabby flesh is decidedly weak.

He'll lead you to his water-bed (bought second-hand, patched with sticking plaster from a more virile previous owner), but it makes him seasick. Next to the bed he keeps a jar of stud cream to persuade his ancient monument to stand erect, but he can't keep it up long enough to perform.

A peek in his bathroom cabinet will reveal Rive Gauche hair gel – look behind, and you'll find the Phyllosan. Don't try to force him into sex – he needs all the beauty sleep he can get. What was a passable male under the disco lights when you were pissed, turns out to be a wrinkled heap of decaying flab in the cold light of day.

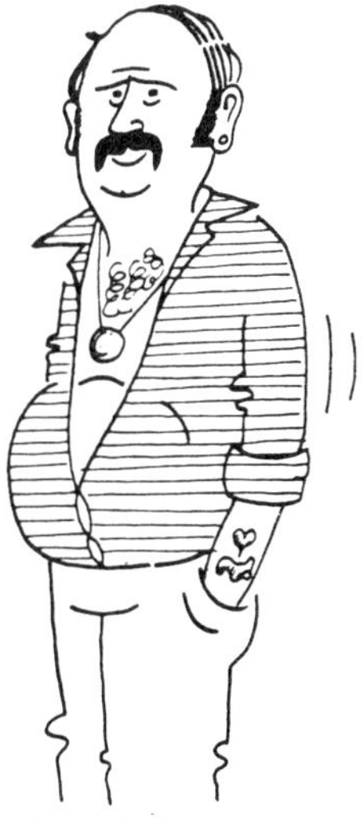

Pros: *The prospect of accompanying him on a cheap Saga holiday to Miami.*

Cons: *He'll never grow old gracefully – he'll be even more of a laughing-stock in ten years' time.*

THE GYNAECOLOGIST

No matter how sexy *you* think your body is, this man will not notice – he's seen it all before. What will turn him on are odd little things like the attractive curve of your fallopian tubes, or the cute contours of your cervix. You can expect foreplay to take the form of a thorough examination, with him wearing latex gloves and you splayed over the dressing table with a reading lamp suitably placed.

He may be quick to find your G-spot, that elusive haven of heavenly feeling, but you can't help wondering if he's comparing you with cross-section illustrations in the latest copy of *The Lancet*. Don't get paranoid – borrow his magnifying glass and insist on an extensive examination of *his* bits and pieces before love-play commences.

If you're into oral sex you may be disappointed – he'll regard it as a waste of those talented, skilful hands and nimble, professional fingers. He considers contraception to be his responsibility and will insist on Safe Sex, which means an extra thick Durex, the equivalent of having a bath with galoshes on. And no sharing-a-joint after-glow with this chappie – it's

£ **The only man you've met who charges for foreplay.**

A pronounced preference for fish restaurants.

The ultimate in clinical sex.

off to the bathroom for an antiseptic swish.

Sex with this man can be a bit of a passion killer; if he produces a Polaroid from his bag of tricks and asks you to pose astride a chair for a full frontal photo – all in the interests of medical science of course – well, tell him to get lost.

Pros: *He can spot a prolapse at a hundred paces, and can advise on your retroverted uterus or incipient ovarian cysts.*

Cons: *His encyclopaedic knowledge of your reproductive system can soon become a bore.*

THE BASTARD

An amazing looker, and knows it, though the cream suit was nicked from an Oxfam shop, the tan came out of a bottle and the impeccable hair owes more to Recital and L'Oréal than it does to nature. A compulsive liar who is incapable of giving more than thirty seconds concentration to any subject other than himself, he can usually be found in the newest trendy nightclub, boring the staff with tales of his latest conquests.

To merit his attention you'll have to be a stereotype stunner: stilt-high heels, high-gloss purple lipstick, spiky eyelashes, thrusting boobs and naughty nipples. He'll whisper a provocative introduction in your ear ('Now you look as though you could do with a real man') and ask you to buy him a drink.

Provided you're attractive enough, he'll allow you to listen to him boasting about his latest dubious business deals, while giving the club regulars the chance to admire his latest lay. If you're nothing special to look at, his eyes will be constantly roving until he's sure there's nothing better available.

Sex will be at your place – he won't want to stain his sheets or let you know where to find him when

£ **Loads, but you won't see any more of it than his ex-wife did.**

You may be allowed the privilege of cooking him a meal, for which he probably won't turn up.

If you're not protected, he'll claim he's had a vasectomy. Why should he waste money on Durex?

you discover he's given you herpes – he has enough problems evading his ex-wife's attempts to get some maintenance money. ('Well she shouldn't have had any bloody kids, should she?').

Screwing – he's never made love in his life – is for his total self-gratification: it's just like doing press-ups except you happen to be underneath. No post-coital chat; he dresses and disappears, leaving you wondering sadly why on earth you did it.

Pros: *At least you won't be under any illusions.*

Cons: *Could put you off men for life.*

THE LONELY HEART

The personal ad reads 'Initially shy, romantic, well-built male, fortyish, no ties, seeks sincere female for enduring relationship'. The reality is somewhat different. 'Initially shy' means he needs a couple of lagers before he gets randy. 'Romantic' – only makes love in the dark. 'Well-built' – vastly overweight. 'Fortyish' – fiftyish. 'No ties' – limited wardrobe. And are *you* the woman he's looking for? For 'sincere', read gullible (you'll need to be to fall for him). And the enduring relationship? A quick screw.

There's no point in asking for a photo when you answer the ad. He'll either send a snap taken ten years ago when he had some hair, or a portrait of his best friend, a Robert Redford lookalike. Advertising for a girlfriend is a sign of desperation, so don't expect miracles. If he's a bachelor, he's probably looking for a mother substitute; if he's divorced, she may have sued for terminal boredom.

Arrange to meet him in a crowded pub after work and give a false description of yourself, so you can beat a hasty retreat if he's a real dog. But don't be

£ **Most of it goes on personal ads, stamps, phone calls, and subscriptions to computer dating agencies.**

Nothing too sophisticated. He's the sort who uses the grapefruit knife to cut his T-bone.

Either a virgin or hasn't found anyone to do it with for years. Odds on he's a premature ejaculator.

fooled by appearances. He may look presentable perched on a bar stool, but when he stands up you'll find he's only five foot tall and his socks don't match.

Lonely Hearts propose, on average, five weeks after the first meeting, so if you want to hitch yourself to a hare-lipped bank clerk on the Club 18-30 blacklist, he's your man.

Pros: *You'll never have to worry about him straying – no one else would look at him.*

Cons: *Can you trust your future happiness to a silicon chip?*

THE LATIN LOVER

With his gleaming white teeth and a gleaming brown tan, the Latin Lover is easily spotted across crowded dance floors in dark discos. The open neck shirt reveals a thick curly carpet, suggesting that every last inch of him is fully fitted. Well dressed and sensual, his slim hips are squeezed into trousers so tight you can see the pimples on his bum – and which leave you in no doubt at all about the size of his organ.

Introducing himself by way of a pinch on the bottom, he turns the most frenetic dance numbers into an excuse for a close-up smooch, thus allowing you a more intimate introduction to the pulsating bulge in his trousers. Whispering garlic-scented romanticisms in a beautifully exaggerated continental accent, he explains that he is a partner in a 'leetle restaurant' – which means he makes the sandwiches in Papa's snack bar.

£ **Not much, but knows how to spend it e.g. well-chosen clothes and yummy, but overpowering, aftershave.**

Cheap but presentable restaurant where he knows the staff, or back to his place to try Mama's spaghetti.

Amazing stamina – the woman usually gives up first. Could give you a few ideas to try out with the Mr Monotonous in your life.

Back to your place, where foreplay begins before you've even had a chance to turn the key in the lock. He says he'd love a coffee, but you are far too distracted to think about turning the kettle on. The romantic chit-chat continues in bed, interspersed with dramatic groans and exaggerated compliments. The relationship won't last, so enjoy those long nights of passion while you can.

Pros: *Good looking, great lover, and has all the chat. A charmer to you, your mother …*

Cons: *… and every other woman. Mind you don't catch something!*

THE MCP

Self-centred and patronising, MCPs can be spotted gathering in cliques at the bar, roaring lustily at very old jokes about women drivers while leering drunkenly at the barmaid's boobs. You'll have been dumped in a corner with the other 'girls', along with sufficient supplies of Snowballs and Babycham to keep you quiet for the evening. He'd have been happier to leave you at home, but thought you might like the opportunity to chat about knitting or to swap a few recipes. When he's well and truly oiled (about an hour after you were ready to go) he'll stagger over and say 'God, aren't you ready to go yet? You girls do like a gossip, don't you?'

Then it's home for the traditional Friday night fuck: three minutes of beery-breathed bonking which finishes the moment he's come. Any ideas of a post-coital cuddle will be abruptly terminated by him falling asleep, or sending you to make him a cup of tea and sandwich. Meanwhile, he'll turn on *Match of the Day* on the bedside telly (his side of course) but may well be fast asleep and loudly snoring by the time you get back with his sandwich.

£ **Don't you worry your little head about money – that's a man's business.**

You won't be allowed to see the menu; if you are, he'll dismiss your choice as unsuitable ('Oh no, you wouldn't like that') and order for you.

Missionary position only: it's his role to dominate and yours to submit. Female orgasm? Never heard of it.

If you've been unwise enough to marry an MCP, be warned: he'll expect you to look demurely pretty at all times, be a Cordon Bleu cook in the kitchen, a whore in the bedroom and a housemaid from Monday to Sunday. He'd be amazed to discover that shirts are not self-ironing, and he thinks a tea towel is something to wipe his hands on when he's finished playing with the car.

If he's still courting you (i.e. showing you off to his friends), you may get taken out for the odd meal. This will be a frustrating experience: your opinions will be ignored or dismissed out of hand, he'll flirt with the waitresses, and at the end of it all he'll expect you to sleep with him. Well, why not – he's spent a lot of money on you.

Pros: *None.*

Cons: *Could put you off men for life.*

THE MACROBIOTIC MAN

The Macrobiotic Man is a truly wholesome person: wholemeal in his diet, wholehearted in his relationships, holistic when it comes to medicine, but hopeless if you fancy a wild weekend of sexual frolics and boozy self-indulgence.

You can spot this man by the good cause badges on his limp lapels, a washed-out logo T-shirt *(I Saved a Tree in '83)*, his Nature Trek shoes and the tell-tale signs of a high fibre diet. His life is a frantic round of save-the-whale rallies and stop-the-motorway sit-downs. If he can spare the time, he may take you to a Friends of the Earth meeting to discuss the imminent extinction of the Maplin Sands Lug Worm, or the threat to the Dartford Warbler from a new American missile base.

When you eventually manage to drag him away for a meal, you'll be given a run down on the E-numbered additives in your prawn cocktail, he'll complain to the waiter that his grapefruit's been irradiated and he'll ask for soya milk in his decaffeinated coffee. Back at his place you'll be treated to a glass of organic parsnip wine before being invited to join him on the futon. Contraception is the rhythm method only; the

£ **Regards money as a nasty capitalist invention, mainly because he hasn't got any.**

Lentil burgers with brown rice.

He's understanding about PMT and female problems in general, and insists on a whole-milk yogurt treatment for that 'feminine itch'.

resulting children will be brought up on the nurture-their-self-expression principle – i.e. let them do whatever they like.

Forget the champagne and post-coital fag – instead, he'll offer a glass of raspberry tea, a lecture on the dangers of cigarettes, and a warning that passive smoking may be giving your budgie bronchitis.

Pros: *Gentle and caring.*

Cons: *Espousing a what-is-natural-must-be-good philosophy means that he cannot be relied on not to fart in front of great-grandmother.*

THE LECHER

He always takes the tube in the rush hour for close encounters of the intimate kind. That's no shopping bag pressing into your posterior – it's the Lecher's ever-ready groin. He's learned to stand without strap-hanging, leaving his wandering hands free for furtive groping.

There's usually one in every office. He can never look you in the eye, he's too busy sizing up your attributes. A thoroughly unsavoury character, easily recognised by beads of perspiration on the upper lip, and tongue running hungrily over his moustache. If you're ever formally introduced, his handshake will be clammy and reptilian; he may even tickle your palm.

He has a ball on New Year's Eve. When everyone else is full of alcohol-induced bonhomie and the good-natured kissing starts, he'll ram his tongue down your throat and insist on a full-blown snog. He loves body contact; dancing with him is like being mauled by a hyperactive octopus. He'll press his slimy body next to yours, subject you to slobbering kisses, and squeeze your buttocks firmly.

Walk past him in a bar and he'll run a sweaty hand over your posterior. Sit next to him and you'll find

£ **He gives a whole new meaning to the term 'filthy lucre'.**

Burger and chips – in fact anything greasy.

If you're desperate enough to go to bed with him, you'll probably find he's impotent.

his trembling thigh pressing meaningfully into yours, and a tarantula-like hand on your knee.

To cope with a Lecher, you'll need night classes in karate, a can of mace in your bag, and a rape alarm at the ready.

Steer clear of him at the office party, or your credibility score will plummet and your chances of promotion will vanish. He's a thoroughly nasty piece of work.

Pros: *His attentions may be useful when you're suffering from PMT and feeling undesirable…*

Cons: *… but once encouraged he's impossible to shake off.*

THE FOOTBALL FANATIC

He never washes or shaves, but he'll spend hours polishing his bovver boots; his hair is dyed in the colours of his favourite team, and if you're really unlucky he'll have a spider's web tattooed on his face. Wears his football scarf every day of the year – except when playing away to Man. Utd. (well, discretion's the better part of valour, in't it?).

Saturdays, he crawls out of bed about midday, just in time to watch *Football Focus* or *Saint and Greavsie*. Then it's off to the pub to get 'well pissed up' before the game. If his team's playing away, you'll be lucky to see him again before Tuesday, though you may get a phone call asking you to bail him and fourteen mates out of a gaol in Wolverhampton.

His hobbies include damaging British Rail property, starting fires on cross-channel ferries and getting thrown out of pubs.

He couldn't tell you the name of the Prime Minister, but he knows the name of every Charlton Athletic goalkeeper since 1901, and that Bert Foggerty missed a penalty in a 1947 cup semi-final at Villa Park. The highlight of his

£ **Borrows money from you to pay his fines.**

Hot dog from a street vendor.

Not the best of lovers, but certainly the noisiest: 'Here we go, here we go, here we go...' Don't expect extra time or a replay.

career was streaking naked across the sacred turf of Wembley stadium during the 1976 Cup Final.

If he ever takes you for a drink on a Saturday (which assumes that *Match of the Day* isn't on), you'll find that all the pubs in the area have been boarded up in anticipation of his arrival. Continental holidays are right out: he's currently wanted by the Belgian police.

Pros: *Has promised to take you to see Millwall in the Cup Final.*

Cons: *Millwall will never get to the Cup Final.*

THE MEANIE

Years of practice have taught this guy how to outfumble everyone else when it comes to dipping into his pocket. And isn't it strange how he always disappears to the gents when it's his round?

If he takes you out for a meal, you can be sure he's checked out the restaurant in advance so he's carrying the only credit card they don't accept. He also keeps an empty cheque book in his inside pocket for emergency use. There's an aura of mothballs about him – he keeps them in his wallet, a calfskin affair bought by his mother for his 12th birthday, still in mint condition.

Watch him cooking breakfast. See the way he switches off the gas while he turns over the bacon? He also makes sure the kettle only holds enough water for each cup, so as not to waste electricity. You'll never see him driving at more than 40 mph. And why does no one sell one-star petrol?

He's easily spotted by his clothes. OK, demob suits are high fashion, but this guy's are original. He never throws anything away in case it becomes chic again, so kipper ties, winkle-pickers and velvet-collared drapesuits are *de rigeur* for evening wear. And can you really get passionate over someone who recycles paper hankies?

£ **Doesn't trust banks, so he keeps it all hidden at home. Has a heart attack at the thought of a burglary.**

Salvation Army soup kitchen.

The only man you know who re-uses Durex.

It's the same story in bed. Why waste energy in steamy love-making when he can conserve it in a Rip van Winkle sleeping session?

You may be the generous type, but this guy will abuse the privilege. One thing's certain: if there's a way of taking it with him when he goes, he'll find it.

Pros: *None.*

Cons: *A life of re-cycled tea bags and un-ironed shirts. 'Well, the cost of electricity you know, it all adds up...'*

THE RED HOT LOVER

His body is flawlessly fit, as befits a guy who gets plenty of press-up practice. Every muscle is honed to perfection, including the love-muscle, the tool of his trade. A well-oiled sex machine with only one life to live, he won't waste time on challenges or time consuming seduction scenes. It's take it or leave it – but show him a willing woman and he'll show you a permanent erection.

Spot him in a disco, eyeing up the talent and drinking slimline tonic water (has to watch his figure and daren't risk brewer's droop). He's a great dancer, wears the latest fashions and is always scrupulously clean. He's equally fussy about his partners and won't waste his body on scrubbers – he prefers disco queens, with sunbed tans and gold chains.

Bang up to date on the latest sex techniques, he hasn't used the missionary position since he was thirteen. You're a slow-starter? Don't worry. He'll find erogenous zones where you didn't know you had a zone at all. His mirror-lined bedroom is packed with stud cream, erection-sustaining penis rings, condoms with special nodules, peach melba flavour douches and vibrators in all shapes and

£ **He's healthy rather than wealthy and he's got lots of expenses – Health club subscriptions, sex manuals, batteries …**

Doesn't need to wine and dine you. But you may get champagne poured over your body for him to lick off.

He's practised so much he's achieved near perfection. But it's a one night stand – and mind you don't catch something.

sizes. He may even treat you to a private screening of the latest Danish sex video.

But don't be fooled – it's a different girl every night. When you're with him, it seems you're the only woman in his life. But he'll only stay faithful for the duration of the sex act – though that may take some time: this one has staying power.

Pros: *He'll give you a night to remember…*

Cons: *… but don't fall in love. You'll only last as long as his erection – though that* ***is*** *quite long…*

THE MARRIED MAN

Easily recognised by his mortgage mentality, frayed cuffs, gravy stained tie and harassed hangdog expression, which turns into a gleeful 'can't believe my luck' schoolboy enthusiasm when he realises you're interested. Another dead giveaway is his car: discarded comics, a smell of baby vomit and a child seat in the boot.

One thing in his favour: married men are grateful for anything they can get. And who says you can't teach an old dog new tricks? He'll be keen to experiment in bed, but will be careful not to flaunt his new-found talents at home. Wearing make up or perfume is a no-no with this one – he'll be paranoid about telltale signs. And no orgasmic backscratching. You'll have to curb your passion or file your nails down to the quick.

If you do fall for him, be prepared to spend weekends, Christmas and Bank Holidays alone while he's in the bosom of his unsuspecting family. He'll expect you to sit by the phone, in your lonely flat, on the off chance that he can snatch a thirty second call. But be warned – this guy is an accomplished liar. He'll tell you his wife doesn't understand him; then you see him with her at the

£ **The mere thought of maintenance payments gives him chronic debtor's droop.**

Scruffy backstreet pubs – he daren't go anywhere he might be recognised.

Enthusiastic – but he's always got an eye on the clock.

window table of a cosy restaurant, enjoying an intimate candlelit dinner. And far from being the old battleaxe he described, she's a Bo Derek lookalike. All *you* get is a bottle of El Cheapo round at your place before getting down to the furtive frolics. And if you're harbouring ideas of becoming a wife – forget it; whatever he says, he'll never leave her.

Pros: *A refreshing change from smooth young men…*

Cons: *… but you'll always play second fiddle.*

THE WIMP

Still a virgin at the age of 29, The Wimp has been tied to his mother's apron strings since the day he was born. His pale complexion owes as much to her cooking as to the various nervous disorders she has convinced him he's suffering from.

His mother still buys all his clothes, dressing him, like his father, from John Collier and Tesco. Occasionally, he gazes wistfully into Chelsea Man, or even Next for Men, but the last time he bought himself a shirt Mummy sent him back to Marks to change it. He's had the same short-back-and-sides since the age of six and always smells vaguely of Vick Vapour Rub.

He asks girls out once a year, to accompany him to the annual cricket club dance. But finding a partner isn't easy: he'll plead with anyone from the mini-skirted office junior to the director's secretary, and finally, in desperation, the check-out girl from Tesco's. They all decline. He once had a girlfriend

£ **Keeps his money in a purse inscribed 'A present from Llanduddno'.**

Mummy thinks eating out is a waste of money, so she'll send him on a date with a pack of meat paste sandwiches and a flask of orange squash. And don't expect to be picked up in a car: The Wimp will have his bus pass.

Hasn't quite grasped the basic gender differences. He knows girls have got bumps on their fronts and that you're supposed to try and kiss them; he's not quite sure what happens after that.

(a spotty lass who worked, of course, in a Wimpy) but his mother said she was common, so she had to go.

The nearest he'll get to wining and dining you will be to offer you an invitation to come home for Sunday tea. He'll take off his shoes when he enters the house and put on his slippers. You'll be fed on ham so thin you could read through it, followed by tinned mandarin oranges and evaporated milk; after tea, you can settle down on the plastic sofa to watch *Stars on Sunday* on the telly. Meanwhile, Mummy will be giving you a searching once over, but no girl will ever be good enough for her little boy.

Pros: *This is one man who* ***won't*** *give you AIDS.*

Cons: *When did you last have to show a guy how to take off your knickers – or have to explain that, no, girls* ***didn't*** *wear Y-fronts?*

NOTES

You will find my idea of

Pete on p50

NICK on p28

BRIAN ON p32

DEREK ON p54

LEO ON p36

ALVIN ON p88

LEE ON p40

JOHN ON p64

MARK ON p32

LINDEN ON p42.

NOTES

INDEX

THE AUTHORS

Chrissie Glazebrook is a freelance writer and broadcaster. She has a weekly show on local radio, and has contributed numerous articles to magazines and newspapers. She lives, loves and works in Yorkshire. **Vanessa Trampleasure** (yes, that *is* her real name) works in public relations and is a part-time writer. Her hobbies include tracing the genealogy of her name – so far back to the 16th century. **Margy Cockburn** (that's *her* real name too) was born and brought up in Liverpool but now lives in London. She boasts a Ph.D in sociology and works as a freelance journalist. **Cathy Murphy** trained to be a teacher but now works in advertising. Her interests include men, drinking, playing Mah Jong and 'ligging' – she has developed gate-crashing into a fine art. **Martin Butcher** has written a number of humorous books, including *The Boozer's Guide to Marriage* and *The Boozer's Guide to Sex*. Unlike Margy Cockburn, he has an extremely bad degree in sociology, and reckons he has learnt a lot more from this book than he has put into it. **'Mollusc'** (Brian West) has produced a wide variety of cartoons and illustrations for newspapers, magazines, books and television. His previous publications include *The Boozer's Late Night Cook Book* and *The Boozer's Guide to Health*.

Also published by Chalk & Cheese Publications:
The Boozer's Guide to Sex
The Boozer's Guide to Marriage
The Boozer's Guide to Health
The Boozer's Late Night Cook Book
My Computer Doesn't Love Me!
The Complete Guide to Rough Golf